Developing
YOUR
Greatness
WITHIN

Because You're Kind of a Really BIG Deal!!

Less than 30 Days Towards a New, Transformed You at Any Age

TRACY RICKS

Developing Your Greatness Within

Printed in the United States of America.

In loving memory of my amazing father, Mr. Lonnie (L.J.) Stallworth, Jr. and my awesome father-in-love, Bishop James R. Ricks, Sr. who both strongly believed in my greatness even when I had a hard time believing in it myself.

TABLE OF CONTENTS

DEDICATION

To my mother, Nettie Stallworth, thank you for always loving and supporting me unconditionally. You and our Daddy always believed in my greatness, even when I didn't believe in it myself. Thanks for pushing me to complete my first book, and forever I am grateful for you. I love and appreciate you dearly!

And to my awesome pastor and husband, Rex Ricks Sr. I thank God that you are unique in every way. You are genuinely comfortable in your greatness. You refuse to follow the crowd and never give in to doing things the way others say they should be done just because "they" say so. You are indeed an original who has been a tremendous example for me, our children, and so many others to follow. I love you and our family more than all the tea in China!

To Christina, Rex Jr., and Tia, the best children on this side of heaven. I am honored to be your mother. Thanks for always supporting and loving me.

INTRODUCTION

Visions and dreams that can change the whole world "trapped" inside an ordinary girl. She looks just like you, but often too afraid to dream out loud!

~ Excerpt from "Never Give Up" by Yolanda Adams

Once upon a time, there was a happy little girl from a small town, but she had big dreams. She and her younger sister would often escape to their *own* world of paper doll land and lived out many of their dreams and fantasies. As they began to grow older, she began to realize that even though many people have dreams, visions, and fantasies, living them out in real life is not always easy. That little girl grew up, and that little girl used to be ME.

I remember vividly how life started feeling hard as I grew older and how my future often seemed bleak and uncertain. I was following the same old routines, barely making it from paycheck to paycheck. I was not happy living an ordinary, mundane life and became very unsure of myself—until the day that I heard a man of wisdom say, "God has an awesome future and destiny for your life!"

At that time, his words were hard to believe. Some people appeared to have all the good fortune while others like me—or so I thought—were sentenced to a life of gloom and doom. Nonetheless, I decided right then and there to do whatever it takes to reach the destiny that man said that God has for me.

Following through on that decision was definitely not easy. I first had to admit that the life I was living was the result of all the choices that I had made. That was a hard pill to swallow, but it enabled me to see that I often made bad choices by default. In the words of Henry Ford, I came to discover that, "Whether we think we can or think we can't, we are right."

I did not know that the life that I wanted for myself was trapped inside of me—in those dreams and visions that I no longer dared to live out. But once I began taking responsibility for my life and aggressively changing what I thought about myself—about my dreams and visions and my circumstances—the entire trajectory of my life changed. I had a total paradigm shift that immediately empowered me to begin developing my greatness. I discovered that fulfilling my destiny is totally up to me. No one, not anyone, could stop me from walking in it — but me! I later learned that my great future was not ahead of me but was hidden on the inside, waiting for me to believe in it.

I often meet many amazing people with great visions and dreams also trapped on the inside of them. If you can relate, I want you to know that this book was written for you. If you feel like I did—if you do not like where you are in your life right now, if you feel stuck, or if you know there is more, this book is just for you. Also, pay close attention because I have hidden some of my **GEM nuggets** throughout the chapters that will also empower you with knowledge for rapid results.

I also included exercises at the end of each chapter, along with a page for your special notes. I pray that as you read, you too will decide to work towards becoming the best version of yourself unapologetically and start living your best life on your terms without limits. No, it's not too late to develop your greatness!

"Wise instruction is like a costly gem. It turns the impossible into success."
(Proverbs 17:8 TPT)

"You have greatness within you and responsibility to manifest that greatness."
~ Les Brown

CHAPTER 1

You Were Born Great!

"Most people search high and wide for the key to success. If they only knew, the key to their dreams lies within."

~ **George Washington Carver**

D id you know that you were made in the very image of God and that you are His workmanship, His masterpiece of art? Ephesians 2:10 says that you are:

"His workmanship [His own masterwork, a work of art], created in Christ Jesus [reborn from above—spiritually transformed, renewed, ready to be used] for good works, which God prepared [for you] beforehand [taking paths which He set]."

The Amplified version goes on to explain that you were created so that you,

"Would walk in them [living the good life, which He prearranged and made ready...]."

He did this for you. Yes—you! God knows you. He made you Himself, and you are His. Isaiah 43:1 says,

"But now, O Jacob, listen to the Lord who created you.
O Israel, the one who formed you says, "Do not be afraid,
for I have ransomed you. I have called you by name;
you are mine."

The New Living Translation says it this way:

"Listen to me, all you in distant lands! Pay attention, you
who are far away! The Lord called me before my birth;
from within the womb he called me by name."

Within the womb, He called you by name. He knows you
by name. You are His most valuable and prized possession.
He refers to you as the apple of His eye, His precious
jewel:

"They shall be Mine," says the Lord of hosts, "On the day
that I make them My jewels. And I will spare them as a man
spares his own son who serves him."
(Malachi 3:17 NKJV).

You are so special to God that He even numbered
every strand of hair on your head. You are so special and
unique that no one has the same fingerprints as yours—not
even your identical twin if you have one.

1 Thessalonians 1:4 (MSG) is also an assurance that
you are not only unique, but God also has something
special that awaits you:

"God not only loves you very much but also has put His
hand on you for something special."

Why Do You Need To Know How Special You Are To God?

So many people are suffering from an identity crisis—not knowing who they are, whose they are, and how valuable they are to God. Knowing your identity is vital to your self-confidence. When you do not know who you are and whose you are, it is easy to let other people tell you who they "think" you are. In other words, society will put labels on you that are simply not true. You may have done what they say you did, but you are not the person they say you are. Once you become aware of who you are in Christ, no longer will you succumb or give in to those degrading labels that are meant to tear down your self-esteem and destroy your self-image.

Others around you may not see it, and you might even find it hard to believe, but you were born with greatness inside. You were born great! And developing the greatness that resides within you and becoming the best version of you—walking in purpose and living the life you want—is a really big deal to God; it is what you were created for, and God Himself fearfully and wonderfully made you. I want you to know that, just like me, your great future is not ahead of you but hidden on the inside waiting for you to believe in it.

"You formed my innermost being, shaping my delicate inside and my intricate outside, and wove them all together in my mother's womb. I thank you, God, for making me so mysteriously complex! Everything you do is marvelously

breathtaking. It simply amazes me to think about it! How thoroughly you know me, Lord! You even formed every bone in my body when you created me in the secret place, carefully, skillfully shaping me from nothing to something. You saw who you created me to be before I became me!"

(Psalm 139:13-16a TPT)

First Nugget: You are a spirit that has a soul that lives inside your body. If you are a believer, your spirit was made alive to God upon your salvation. In this book, you will learn how to work on your soul [your mind, your will, your emotions] which is often neglected. I have found that most believers go from one extreme – super spiritual – to another extreme – totally relying on themselves and their works with no balance between the two. My prayer is that upon the completion of this book, you will learn to develop your greatness and start living your best, balanced life as your soul prospers.

"Beloved, I pray that you may prosper in all things and be in health, just as your soul prospers."

(3 John 1:2 NKJV)

Exercise:

1) Take a few minutes and meditate on how special you are to God.

2) What would you like to see manifest in your life upon completion of the reading of this book? Write it down.

_____

_____

_____

_____

_____

_____

_____

_____

_____

_____

_____

_____

Notes...

CHAPTER 2
Believing in Your Greatness

"To build self-esteem, you have to outface your negative beliefs about yourself and change them."

~ Asmaa Dokmak

Recognizing that you are God's work of art, predestined for something special, is the first step towards developing the greatness within you. Did you know that what you believe about yourself sets the course of your life? Your beliefs and the thoughts you have about yourself guide the decisions you make, either paralyzing you or propelling you forward. Your life today is the sum total of the choices you have made, and those decisions reflect what you've been thinking and believing about yourself.

"You can rationalize it all you want and justify the path of error you have chosen, but you'll find out in the end that you took the road to destruction."

(Proverbs 14:12 TPT)

In the book of Proverbs, there's a scripture that says, *"As a man thinketh in his heart, so is he."* In other words, your mindset directly influences your destiny. You are the author of your own life story and having the right mindset about yourself directly impacts your destiny. I know this is true from my personal experience. I had countless people tell me that I was destined for greatness, but it wasn't until I began believing in the greatness within me that the trajectory of my life changed for the better.

In the account of the spies sent to check out the Promised Land in Exodus, the Bible shows how this truth plays out. The majority of those sent to spy out the land came back to report that while the land was indeed flowing with milk and honey just as the Lord had said, but they could not overtake it. Why? According to their own words recorded in Exodus 13:33, *"There are giants in the land. We are like grasshoppers in their eyes."* This "grasshopper mentality" kept all but two of them, Joshua and Caleb, from possessing the Promised Land. Joshua and Caleb gave a different report. Perhaps you're thinking like I did, what made Caleb and Joshua's report so different from the rest? Why did they have the confidence to take the land?

Possessing a Different Spirit

The scripture says Caleb and Joshua "had a different spirit." I submit to you that people with a different spirit think differently about themselves. They have the right view of themselves in that they think highly of themselves—just not more highly than they ought to think.

Romans 12:3 says, *"do not think of yourself more highly than you ought, but rather think of yourself with sober judgement."* Contrary to the other spies, what Joshua and Caleb thought about themselves and their ability to overtake the land was right.

Psychologists agree that your level of self-esteem—how much you like, respect, and how you feel about yourself is a crucial determining factor of how successful you will be in any area of your life. The ability to think highly of yourself—having "positive self-esteem"—originates mostly from your perception of your own ability to master life, achieve goals, perform tasks, and get the results expected—what psychologists call "self- efficacy." Noted Psychologist Albert Bandura referred to self-efficacy as the mind's self-regulatory function because it tells you when to try and when to stop. If you do not believe something is possible for you to do, you are not likely to attempt it and more likely to give up early, if you even dare try at all. This also proves that procrastination is not a behavior problem but a direct result of negative self-esteem issues.

Here's another Nugget: The way we think determines the way we feel. The way we think, and feel will determine whether we are going to take action or not. Example: If you have a poor self-image and you think you aren't good enough, you will start feeling bad about yourself which will cause you to put that project [that you've been trying to start for weeks] on hold one more day. This behavior is also known as procrastination and as a result stops you from taking any necessary action. I have seen many who have tried to change this type of behavior with no success. Sadly, they are unaware that it's their thinking about themselves – their low self-esteem/self-efficacy – that's causing this problem and holding them back.

Your self-efficacy comes from the type of attention that you received as a child—from both the verbal and nonverbal cues that you were given by family, friends, and even your environment—whether consciously or subconsciously. The strokes or type of attention that you did or did not receive as a child has a significant impact on your ability to become an emotionally healthy adult.

That's why one of my pet peeves is family members and friends that tease others about their looks or other things that cannot be controlled. Such teasing can cause a person to grow up with insecurities that may keep them from moving forward in their life. I know a lady who is 40 years old and still afraid to change her hairstyle because her family members teased her about having a big forehead throughout her childhood. Even though it wasn't true, it became her truth and has kept her in bondage concerning her hair. I know another young lady who has always wanted to start a business but is afraid to try because her high school guidance counselor told her that she was not smart enough, and specifically that she was not good enough in math to open a business. After many years of being out of high school, those harsh words still ring fresh in her mind and has paralyzed her from even trying to step out on her dream of becoming an entrepreneur.

Verbal and nonverbal validations and recognition during childhood confirm a person's self-worth. Positive strokes that express affection, warmth, or appreciation—whether verbally or with a look, touch, smile, or gesture—are essential, life-giving, and good fuel for your psyche in the same way that good food is fuel for your body.

Conversely, negative strokes can damage your self-worth and cause low self-esteem. Have you ever met someone very smart and beautiful but suffers from low self-esteem? I would submit to you that most of the time, their environment shaped their lack of belief in themselves. Everyone needs positive psychological strokes as a child because it forms the foundation for loving yourself as an adult.

If you grew up in an environment that was not necessarily bad but was not conducive for developing your greatness, more than likely you have some thoughts and beliefs about yourself that are limiting your self-worth and causing you to see yourself as a grasshopper in one manner or another. Now don't be hard on yourself because none of us grew up in a perfect environment with perfect parents, an ideal family, or all great friends. This is something that we all must face. **Nugget:** Anything that we are not willing to confront we can never conquer.

Question: Are there things about yourself that you do not like? Do you sometimes feel unworthy? Maybe you doubt your abilities. You are not alone! Mostly everyone is susceptible to feeling like that at one time or another. Having those thoughts is not what makes you different or somehow less, but it's how you deal with those thoughts and beliefs. In the words of Eleanor Roosevelt, "No one can make you feel inferior without your consent." I pray that you see that it's not you but the thoughts and beliefs that you have about yourself that are holding you back from realizing the greatness within you.

To be successful and start developing your greatness, you must first like yourself and decide to start believing in you. Sometimes you just have to start believing in yourself by faith.

In other words, you must choose to believe in the greatness within you despite what you may think or feel right now. You can start by accepting yourself just as you are, without condemning yourself for any shortcomings. Begin talking to yourself like you would talk to someone you love. Tell yourself, "I can do this," "I got this," "I'm more than enough," If you can't believe in your own words, start by believing and confessing what God says about you: "I am fearfully and wonderfully made." "Yes, I can do all things through Christ who strengthens me."

You are never too young or too old to start believing in you and start developing your greatness. You can change what you believe and how you think about yourself—and, in so doing, change your whole life. **Nugget:** Anything learned can be re-learned. With a "different spirit"—overall healthy self-esteem and self-efficacy — you will start feeling good about yourself, believing in you, and re-defining yourself even though you may have been broken and have imperfections just like the rest of us.

I have found that too many people have very low self-efficacy when it comes to believing in themselves. They believe in others and can support everybody else. Some say they even believe in God but find it hard to believe in themselves. What about starting to believe in that awesome person looking back at you in the mirror right now?

Here's another Nugget: Did you know that out of the millions of sperm cells released during intercourse, your specific egg was the one that connected with the "one" sperm cell that made it through for your conception even to take place? You are indeed one in a million. This is evidence that your life is not a mistake, regardless of what your parents and those around you may say or think. You were born on purpose for a specific purpose. Please know that walking in your destiny, fulfilling your purpose, developing your greatness, and living the life you want is a really big deal to God! There is only one thing that can stop you from receiving His big plans for you and your life—not believing it for yourself.

I urge you to no longer allow your negative thoughts to cause you to doubt yourself and keep you from moving forward. If you are serious about developing your greatness, becoming the best version of you, and starting to live your very best life, you must decide to possess a different spirit too.

Exercise:

Write down three key points that stood out to you in this chapter:

_____

_____

_____

_____

_____

_____

_____

_____

_____

_____

_____

_____

Notes...

CHAPTER 3

The Need for Change

*"The world as we have created it is a process of
our thinking, it cannot be changed without
changing our thinking."*

~ **Albert Einstein**

Y ou may know someone like Terry. She could not
receive any positive strokes about herself and
found it hard to receive compliments from others
because she would continually and unconsciously put
herself down with self-deprecating remarks. When given a
sincere compliment, Terry would find ways to play it down
or make a joke of it because of her self-sabotaging talk and
thoughts about herself, which convinced her that she was
undeserving. If she was the focus of positive attention or
received any display of affection, tenderness, or care, she
became uncomfortable, yet she easily stored up critical
remarks and often felt depressed. It is not a surprise that she
grew up in a household where she became accustomed to
hearing mostly negative remarks and criticism.

To move forward, Terry became aware of how she discounted herself by declining the positive remarks offered by others and decided to consciously change her reaction and behavior. I helped her to uncover what it was about her sense of value and worth that caused her to be uncomfortable receiving compliments. After reflecting on her life, especially her early childhood, we discovered why she developed this unhealthy reaction.

When you grow up in a negative environment, that environment begins to grow up in you. Just like fish cannot survive in a dirty tank, you cannot thrive and develop your greatness in a negative environment. Research shows that a person usually decides on a fixed paradigm around the ages of seven or eight years old, and there is a tendency to remain fixed on those beliefs unless a conscious decision is made to change.

The first time I heard the word "paradigm," I was somewhat mesmerized. I had no clue what it meant, but it sounded interesting. I learned that a paradigm is a multitude of thoughts and habits that are fixed in your subconscious mind. It is the sum total of what you've learned from your very first life experiences and impressions—your core beliefs about yourself and your world around you. Your paradigm reflects the mark that your earliest childhood experiences and interpretations of those experiences left on you. Those thoughts and memories are the cause of your present life reality. That means that to change your life, you must decide to change your paradigm.

Changing your paradigm from a negative or unhealthy mindset is such an important thing to do for yourself because your thoughts and beliefs can be positive and bring out your greatness, or your thoughts and beliefs can be negative and bring you frustration and also causing low self-esteem. A person with an unhealthy mindset focuses primarily on thinking negative, is often closed and refuses to change. Let me give you a few examples of what I mean by an unhealthy mindset:

- *Always focuses on the negative.*

No matter what happens that is good; an unhealthy mindset focuses on the negative or what's lacking. For example, a husband may wash the clothes, cook dinner and mop the floor, but his wife, who has an unhealthy mind is upset because he did not take out the trash. It's hard for a person with an unhealthy mindset to be grateful.

- *Easily and quickly jumps to conclusions.*

Despite having no evidence, an unhealthy mindset assumes the worse. For example, a person with an unhealthy mindset will take offense when another person doesn't say hello, assuming that person meant to insult or disregard them. Those with an unhealthy mindset often see themselves as the victim.

- *Minimizes their positive traits.*

An unhealthy mindset cannot receive compliments. For example, when someone admires what a person with an unhealthy mindset is wearing, they will say, "Oh, this is old" or "This is nothing" instead of simply saying, "Thank you." People with an unhealthy mindset often have a false sense of humility.

- *Discounts others.*

Always seeking approval, an unhealthy mindset fixates on keeping up appearances and getting attention, but then quickly discredits those who admire them. For example, a young lady with an unhealthy mindset will go to great lengths to get the interest of a gentleman, only to reject him when he asks her on a date. A person with an unhealthy mindset often devalues themselves and those who care about them.

- *Treats thoughts and feelings as facts.*

Happy one minute then angry or sad the next, an unhealthy mindset is affected by any and every thought that comes to mind. A person with an unhealthy mindset will act irrationally because they thought or assumed something that caused their feelings to spiral out of control. For example, a wife with an unhealthy mindset may leave her marriage just because she thinks and therefore feels like her husband doesn't really love her—despite him telling her that he loves her over and over. A person with an unhealthy mindset is ruled by their emotions—emotionally weak, unstable, and unreliable.

- *Becomes overly demanding.*

Unrealistic expectations are another hallmark of an unhealthy mindset. For example, a person with an unhealthy mindset will often make blanket statements like, "You should…" or "You have to…" A husband with an unhealthy mindset may tell his wife, "You must cook dinner every day if you want to be a good wife to me." A person with an unhealthy mindset tends to take others for granted.

- *Labels people.*

An unhealthy mindset puts "people in boxes" and generalizes. For example, a person with an unhealthy mindset may claim, "All men are bad," "You can't trust anybody," "Blacks are bad people," "All whites are racist," "She is lazy," and will make comments like, "I'm dumb." A person with an unhealthy mindset is critical of themselves and often becomes critical of others.

- *Takes things personally.*

To an unhealthy mindset, everything that happens is a reflection of themselves. If their child gets low grades or gets into trouble at school, the parent with an unhealthy mindset automatically assumes it's because they are a terrible parent. A wife with an unhealthy mindset will believe it's her fault when her husband cheats. And when a pastor teaches on forgiveness, those in the church with an unhealthy mindset think that they are personally being targeted. An unhealthy mindset makes it difficult to deal with the real issue at hand.

These are just some of the signs of an unhealthy mindset. Most of us have experienced at least some of these and are likely still working on overcoming them. Don't feel bad if this is you, just know that it's time for a change and that you can in fact change. And I am here to help you.

Deciding to Change

I want to stop here to stress the fact that you can indeed change. I say this because once you decide to change, there will be voices that will try to convince you that you don't need to take changing seriously or that you can't change. These voices may come from friends, family, or co-workers—but more importantly, will also come from that voice or inner critic inside your head. Let me first make this very clear: I'm not talking about voices associated with being diagnosed as mentally ill. I'm talking about that nagging, condemning voice that mostly everyone has, which comes from a mindset focused on negative thoughts—those thoughts that don't serve you or me well.

Please make no mistake: Allowing any of these voices—especially your inner critic—keep you from deciding not to deal with an unhealthy mindset can be very, very dangerous. Why? Because it makes you vulnerable to:

- *Aborting your destiny.*

I used to have a bad habit of thinking negative thoughts about myself. It left me having to fight off feelings of inadequacy. When I first started my daily Facebook Live videos, I was terrified and so tempted to quit. I was only able to push pass the fear because I had started working on my mindset. I speak from experience when I say that negative feelings cause insecurity and inferiority that can stop you from pursuing God's plan and purpose for your life. When you have a hard time seeing yourself the way God sees you, it's almost impossible to walk out God's great purpose for your life.

- *Destroying valuable relationships.*

You likely know of someone who is unable to make allowances for differences and will even condemn those whom they say they care about; these broken people often use words as weapons of mass destruction. They may slander their mate with false accusations like, "You're cheating on me" or "You don't love me." They will tell friends, "You are damaged goods." After hearing such hurtful words over and over, their loved ones are left nursing wounds and are forced to end the relationship. Toxic, destructive words come from the toxic thoughts that hurt that individual and often causes them to hurt other people—especially those they love the most.

- *Isolating yourself.*

Life was meant to be enjoyed with others. That's why the prison system uses isolation as a punishment. Interactions with others help you see different perspectives, grow, and have the support needed to realize your greatness within. But if you are saying things like, "I can't trust anybody" and come to believe that no one likes or understands you, then you will not be open to receiving help or even just enjoying life with others. Isolation often leads to the devastation of your greatness within.

- *Being crippled by guilt and shame.*

Have you ever thought, "I better not share that with anybody, or they will think I'm a bad person"? Do you feel guilty about your past? These kinds of thoughts put limits on the type of conversations that you're likely to have with those who care the most about you—a healthy dialogue can help you change for the better, boost your self-confidence and provide emotional support. Self-condemnation keeps you from letting friends and family get close, robbing you of feeling accepted.

- *Accepting less.*

It has been proven that a person will never earn 10% more or less than what they subconsciously believe. If you just accept that what you have now is the best that life has to offer you—if you believe that earning more money is out of reach, you will stay in lack. Thinking that you cannot become better and that you are not worth more, is dangerous to the greatness within you because it will stop you from pressing forward, getting the help you may desperately need, and continuing to grow by learning and doing new things.

- *Creating dis-ease.*

Negative thoughts cause negative emotions that can weaken the immune system, leaving you more susceptible to colds, flu, coronavirus, and various other diseases. For example, being angry can cause a stroke, nervous breakdown, and even heart attacks. Also, meditating on negative thoughts often leads to depression, one of many psychosomatic illnesses that occur when the mind [psycho] makes the body [soma] sick. If you want to become sick, keep entertaining negative thoughts about how bad your life is, and keep believing that you are worthless.

- *Contemplating suicide.*

Proverbs 13:12 says, "Hope deferred makes the heart sick, but a longing fulfilled is a tree of life." If you believe that the things in your life cannot get any better and focus on that misconception, you will feel alone and be open to accepting the lie that you are beyond help and that your life is no longer worth living. I want you to know that's a lie! Don't forsake the greatness with you!

If you are battling depression and having suicidal thoughts, please call the National Suicide Prevention Lifeline at 1-800-273-8255, or contact me at hello@tracyricks.com. I'm here to help, and that's what this book and my courses are designed to do. Please do not be afraid to reach out for help. **Nugget:** Seeking help is a sign of strength—not weakness. God, Himself, declares that He is,

"Our refuge and strength, A very Present help in trouble."
(Psalm 46:1 NKJV)

He also says,

"Let us therefore come boldly to the throne of grace that we may obtain mercy and find grace to help in time of need."
(Hebrews 4:16 NKJV)

God Himself, Your Creator, offers help, which implies that at times both you and I need it! We can always seek God for help and also never be afraid or embarrassed to reach out to others. I am a living witness that God also has people equipped to help overcome any of these symptoms we have discussed; I am one of them.

If you're experiencing any of these symptoms, I am urging you to please make a decision now to begin changing your paradigm. **Nugget:** It's okay not to be okay, but it's just not okay to stay that way. Yes, you can decide right now to become proactive and tenacious about thinking and believing positively about yourself based on what God says about you and your life. Please know once again, you are a very big deal to God.

"What is the value of your soul to God? Could your worth be defined by an amount of money? God doesn't abandon or forget even the small sparrow he has made. How then could he forget or abandon you? What about the seemingly minor issues of your life? Do they matter to God? Of course they do! So you never need to worry, for you are more valuable to God than anything else in this world."

(Luke 12:6-7 TPT)

No matter what your inner critic is telling you right now, the task of developing your greatness, becoming the very best version of yourself, and living the life you want is very doable and very possible. Again, I am a living witness!

"But Jesus looked at them and said to them, with men this is impossible, but with God all things are possible."

(Matthew 19:26 NKJV)

Exercise:

Write down any self-sabotaging thoughts or outdated beliefs that have held you down or paralyzed you in your past.

_____

_____

_____

_____

Now replace those thoughts with positive affirmations. For example, if you have thoughts like, "I am not smart enough" then write down "I am smart enough" and begin to repeat it at least three times a day. It has been proven that if you try to empty your mind of negative thoughts but fail to replace them with positive thoughts, the negative thoughts will surely return.

_____

_____

_____

_____

"Death and life are in the power of the tongue, and those who love it will eat its fruit."

(Proverbs 18:21 NKJV)

Notes...

CHAPTER 4

Choose to Change

"Change is painful, but nothing is as painful as staying stuck somewhere you don't belong."

~ Mandy Hale

For years I watched many people who truly believed that every new year was going to be "their year." After hearing, "This is your year" in almost every New Year's Eve service year-after-year, I began to realize that something wasn't right. Most of the people saying this, year after year, only quoted it at the very start of the year while going on to live defeated or just mundane lives the remainder.

Well, sadly, so many of these people continue to pray and think like this year after year without ever seeing the results they want in their lives. You may have heard this definition of insanity – doing the same thing expecting different results. I have met so many who are just waiting on God to wave a wand and change things for them. They will make excuses saying things like, "God is in control". They are frustrated because they believe that God can do it and are just hoping and praying that one day He will.

Although God's will for you is that you realize your greatness, it is your will, your beliefs that determine your life. If you want to develop your greatness and start living your very best life, you have to take responsibility for your own life. I can hear you asking, "How do I take responsibility for my life?"

You start by deciding to change. You can decide today to change and be free to be you and do you, or you can "decide not to decide" and keep living by default. Either way, it's a choice. Life is choice driven. God, Himself said in Deuteronomy 30:19, "*I have set before you life and death, blessings and curses, now choose life that you and your children may live.*" You can choose to decide to change your paradigm and become the best version of you. And then stick with it. **Nugget:** You don't get in life what you hope for, you get in life what you choose to go for.

Let me warn you that changing and having a different spirit—overall healthy self-esteem and self-efficacy—is not something that you can achieve overnight. Your mind is like a giant muscle; you must decide and commit to developing it and re-programming it every single day. Re-programming an unhealthy mindset is vital to developing your greatness and living your very best life. That is why the Bible, in Romans 12:2 says, "*Be ye transformed by the renewing of your mind....*" Notice that this verse says that you are to renew your mind. *You* must change it. So many people are trapped and frustrated because they don't understand that they must renew their "own" mind before they can walk in God's perfect will for their lives and become the best version of themselves.

Also, in this verse the word "Renewing" is a gerund, which means this is a continual process. In other words, renewing the mind is a daily and ongoing thing—never-ending. One of the definitions for the word "renewing" in the original language of the Bible refers to renovation. You must take it upon yourself to renovate or tear down your old paradigm of outdated beliefs, just like someone who renovates a home. Builders often first tear down the old and begin developing the new plan.

Your mind is like a garden. You must plant what God says about you in your heart and cultivate your dreams, visions, and desires in your mindset. You must also continually uproot misconceptions and negativity—the weeds and debris that have taken root from your early years (your old paradigm) and those that come anew. According to statistics, 90% of our thoughts about ourselves are often very negative. So you must learn how to replace them.

Did you know that you decide your fate by what you cultivate in your subconscious mind? Any thought that we plant and cultivate in our subconscious mind, whether good or bad, will one day become a reality. Just as you cannot live your best life when your physical body is out of shape and unhealthy, you cannot effectively develop your greatness within and live your best life holding on to an unhealthy mindset. The decision is totally up to you.

The Word of God explains how this is a decision we must make and how once again it is totally up to us, *"that you put off, concerning your former conduct, the old man which grows corrupt according to the deceitful lusts, and be renewed in the spirit of your mind* (Ephesians 4:22-23 NKJV). **Nugget:** Don't panic, I have some very good news, if you are a believer, you're not going to change by your own might, but we have the Helper, Holy Spirit as our amazing aid.

I remember wavering, being up and down up and down in my own beliefs. Sometimes I would stand strong in faith—believing in the greatness within me. Other times, when life became tough or people who I trusted would say discouraging words; I'd feel myself waver because I had not adequately dealt with my old paradigm. I would stop cultivating the garden of my mind, which caused me to live my life by default. God's Word calls this being "double minded." It's easy to see why James 1:7-8 warns, "let not a double-minded man think he will receive anything from the Lord". Either you will believe in the greatness within you, or you will believe the negative thoughts planted in your mind by Satan, family, friends, life's circumstances, or that critical inner voice. If you choose to believe the negative thoughts that is what will manifest in your life rather than the good plans God has for you. *"For I know the plans I have for you,"* says the Lord. *"They are plans for good and not for disaster, to give you a future and a hope."* (Jeremiah 29:11 NLT) This is also why what you believe about yourself is much more important than what anyone else in your life believes about you.

"The moment of enlightenment is when a person's dreams of possibility become images of probabilities."

~ Vic Bearden

I have met many who are frustrated and discouraged because they believe that God can do the impossible—but just not for them. Their paradigm—their negative subconscious unbelief—is holding them hostage. You may never want to admit it, but maybe deep down inside you do not *believe* in "the God" on the inside of you. Perhaps you don't believe you are worthy or that you are good enough. That unbelief could be what's been hindering the manifestation of the things that you have been praying for and blocking you from receiving the results you so badly desire in your life. That's why God's Word says,

"And no one puts new wine into old wineskins; or else the new wine will burst the wineskins and be spilled, and the wineskins will be ruined."

(Luke 5:37 NKJV).

Whether you are a believer and trust God or not, this principle holds true. You must see yourself differently to have different results in your life. You have to develop a different spirit.

God's will is for you to realize your greatness, but it is your will—your paradigm—that determines your life. In Him, there are no limits to your greatness. Jesus is recorded as saying in Mark 9:23-24,

"'If you can believe, all things are possible to him who believes." Immediately the father of the child cried out and said with tears, "Lord, I believe; help my unbelief!"

Have you ever noticed that this is the only time in the account of Jesus' life where He did not meet the need? I have found that many people believe in their hearts but need help overcoming the unbelief [doubt] in their minds.

If you're like the father to whom Jesus was speaking, I encourage you to stop waiting on God to change your mind for you. Developing your greatness is a decision that only you can make and do. Your decision to embrace a new positive way of thinking will result in a whole new beginning for your life, which is really a big deal to God!

"If you don't change your beliefs, your life will be like this forever. Is that good news?"

~ Dr. Robert Anthony

You can begin today by starting to believe in yourself, shift your paradigm, and start discovering more effective ways of being, talking, and thinking about yourself as you develop your greatness. You are the author of your own life story and having the right mindset about yourself, directly influences your choices and ultimately your destiny.

"The senseless fool treats life like a joke, but the one with living understanding makes good choices."

(Proverbs 15:21 TPT)

I can assure you that once you take it upon yourself to renew your "own" mind, you will begin to become the best version of you and start seeing the results that you want and living your best life. The power to change—to achieve greatness—is within reach right now—right within you. I encourage you to decide to tap into that greatness.

Nugget: There is only one thing that can stop you from receiving His big plans for you and your life, that is "you not believing it for yourself." Like the prayer of Jabez in the Bible, ask God to enlarge your territory—your mental capacity to receive the great life He has provided for you!

"...Oh, that You would bless me indeed, and enlarge my territory..."

(1 Chronicles 4:10 NKJV)

You can decide to start over right now with a whole new perspective about you—choosing to change the way you interpret your life's circumstances and situations, no matter how bad it may seem at this moment.

"The task is not to see a new world but to see the world with new eyes. The person who can change the way they view their world will win without fail."

~ Gerry Robert

Exercise:

Write down one change that you will make and the date you will begin. Start with one permanent positive change at a time. For example, I decided that I would change my attitude and response to others first. I became aware of giving people the wrong response, and I started practicing how to catch myself and pause before responding rather than just reacting out of my emotions.

_____

_____

_____

_____

_____

_____

_____

_____

_____

_____

Notes...

_____

_____

_____

_____

_____

_____

_____

_____

_____

_____

_____

_____

_____

_____

CHAPTER 5

The Stages for Permanent Change

"People want change but won't change."

~ **Rex A. Ricks, Sr.**

Once I decided to change, I became tenacious and very aggressive about achieving the kind of permanent and positive changes that I knew were necessary for developing my greatness and becoming the best version of me. This is also my prayer for you, so let me share with you how I began to see rapid radical results.

First, I set my mind on becoming the new me. This was non-negotiable, so I didn't share my decision with anyone that I knew would have negative comments or those who were known as a "Debbie Doubter" or "Negative Nancy."

Stage 1: Contemplation

Everything starts with a simple thought that you consciously choose to take hold of. To change permanently and positively, you must make a concrete, "solid" decision to develop your greatness. You must become aware of the need for change and set your mind to doing it, refusing to stay the same.

Stage 2: Preparation

Next, I prepared myself to change. I began to read and study lots of material, gathering information on what God says about me in His Word and listening to God concerning areas that I needed to change so I could chart my transformation journey. I thought about what I really wanted in my life, how I wanted to live, and what I wanted out of life. I gave myself permission to dream big again. I wrote all that down so that I had it on paper. This helped to commit the permanent and positive change that I wanted to see in me to my memory and keep it at the forefront of my thoughts. Maybe you've heard the popular expression, "If you stay ready, you don't have to get ready." It simply means to be proactive in preparing so that when it's time to take action, you can.

Then, I began using visualization and affirmations to re-program and renew my mind. I started imagining the new me—doing "Mindercises", reciting confessions and positive affirmations at least three times a day along with doing visualization exercises at least twice a day. **Nugget:** Visualization plus affirmations equal manifestation.

Stage 3 - Part A: Visualization

When you visualize an act, your brain generates an impulse that tells your neurons to "perform" that movement. This creates a new neural pathway, which is a group of cells in your brain that begin working together to create the behavior. This sets your body up to act in a way that's consistent with what you've imagined.

What's so amazing is that all of this occurs without you actually performing the physical activity. Your subconscious mind doesn't know the difference between what is real and what is fantasy. Your subconscious mind interprets the things that you have imagined as though these were real-life actions.

Don't believe me? Well, have you ever watched a movie and started feeling all the emotions as if you were there, going through that experience? Like with that movie, you must see and feel like the "new and positive" you before those positive changes will manifest in your life. **Nugget:** If you can see it, you can be it. The only limitation is your imagination. Once you begin to visualize your change with emotions, acting like it's already done, you will begin to "see" it becoming your new reality.

I found an example of this in the Bible. God told Abram to look at the multitude of stars in the sky when He was assuring Abram of the children he would have. God was saying, "Keep this image before you." Why? Because Abram's wife Sara was old and barren at the time. Abram needed an image to keep in mind even when it didn't look like God's promise was coming to pass in his life.

What I found so interesting is that in Hebrew, the word "image" is translated as "yetser," which means to conceive. Like Abraham, you and I also need a point of reference. If you want to change any old image of yourself that you do not like, you need an image or point of conception. You must use your imagination. **Nugget:** Even in the natural, once a woman conceives, delivery takes place in the near future.

Another interesting fact that I learned is that our brain was created with a reticular activating system [RAS]. This system filters out information that you don't need and helps let in the information that you do need. God designed your brain this way to help bring to your attention what matters most to you, based on your goals and interests— including what you've imagined. For example, once you consider buying a red sports car, you will start seeing red sports cars everywhere. It's not that they were not already on the road, but now your personal RAS is bringing them to your attention. Isn't God awesome!

Once I started visualizing the greatness within me and affirming that greatness with emotions, my RAS started helping me bring that greatness to fruition. I started seeing more and more results. I noticed that the people and things that I visualized and was affirming daily were being drawn to me. All the things that I needed to reach my goals were becoming obvious.

Stage 3 – Part B: Affirmation

Affirmations are formal declarations affirming and speaking your intentions and beliefs to yourself. When using affirmations, you say them over and over with emotion, locking them into your subconscious mind. By so doing, you are re-programming any old, barricaded beliefs and your old paradigms through autosuggestion. Again, please note that whatever we plant into our subconscious mind and nourish it with repetition and emotion will one day become our reality.

There was a woman in the Bible who had an issue of blood for many years. When she heard about Jesus, the Scriptures say, she said to herself, "If I may touch the hem of His garment, I know I will be made whole." One of the translations states that she kept affirming to herself the results she expected to see come to pass in her life and guess what? It happened exactly as she confessed and affirmed it; finally, she was made whole!

In addition to what you see or visualize, your brain learns from what you hear. New neural pathways are also created for every thought you think about and focus your attention on. And when you repeat something that you've heard, it becomes even more imprinted in your subconscious mind. If you are always hearing negative reports, you will eventually start to express these thoughts and opinions. By so doing, you are learning to react in a negative and self-destructive manner. You are creating or reinforcing a paradigm that is opposed to your greatness and your God-given dreams and aspirations.

The Bible says in Proverbs 18:21 that death and life are in the power of the tongue. Because I was prepared, I knew what God said about me and I only confessed what He said about me. Once again, I also knew that whatever we believe and speak daily with conviction and repetition, becomes our reality. So I began affirming my greatness, confessing the Word of God, confessing who I am and Whose I am. For example, I declared that "I am blessed in the country and in the city," even when my life seemed to be going in the opposite direction. That was when my life began to radically change for the best.

Affirmations should always be in the present tense and positive, repeated with emotion, if you want to develop your greatness and see results. Your subconscious mind only takes orders in the present tense—not commands for the future. For example, you should declare, "I am the head and not the tail," instead of "I am going to be the head and not the tail." Never say, "I am going to be great one day," because that hinders your results. As Hebrews 1:11 says, "**Now** faith is [present tense] the substance of things hoped for, the evidence of things not seen."

Next, I began implementing all the new information that I had learned, making a daily choice to walk in my greatness without allowing myself to doubt my greatness or feel the need to prove it to anybody.

Stage 4: Implementation

This is the stage when you start practicing and implementing your new changes and walking in your greatness.

During this stage, I remember being tested by people who were speaking lies about me and had even started spreading slanderous rumors about me to others. My old paradigm—the old Tracy—wanted to defend, retaliate, and state my case or prove my point. But because I had been working daily on creating a healthy mindset by doing "Mindercises", I cried but passed that test with grace. I remained calm, serene, and very peaceful. I even shocked my old self!

Because I developed—and continue to develop my greatness, I have re-defined myself and no longer give my power away to anyone. Now I am finally free to be unapologetically me, after many years of needing the approval and acceptance of others.

"So if the Son makes you free, then you are unquestionably free."
(John 8:36 AMP)

Now, having done my all, I choose to stand and walk in my greatness. This certainly doesn't mean that I don't fall at times, but I choose to consistently get back up even though it's not always easy. I am now hitting the mark more than missing it.

Stage 5: Dedication

Life is choice driven. You can choose to change permanently and positively by making a conscious decision each moment of every single day to stay committed to the process.

I made my decision right from the start. I had a vision and a goal in mind—to develop and walk in my new greatness, to become the best version of me with a completely new and healthy mindset every day.

I am now dedicated to maintaining the new re-defined me, my developed greatness. I will never return to that "old woman and her deeds." I choose to hold on to my new self-image without wavering. Now, whenever I go through challenges, I know how to "grow" through them because of my new healthy mindset. **Nugget:** There is something to learn in every adversity. No, I'm not perfect, but I am getting better every day and in every way. And so can you!

Each of these steps represents a daily, ongoing choice that you must make to establish a healthy mindset by changing your old paradigm. A choice to do as God's Word says and take off the old person that you are and those deeds and put on your new man. If you are tired and want it to finally be "your year" you must decide to transform into your new person by developing your greatness and becoming the best version of you!

I have seen many people try to change their behavior without changing their subconscious mind (those outdated beliefs and old paradigms) – this will not cause permanent positive change. Any progress they seem to make only ends up being temporary. You may hear them say, "I love God, but you can still catch these hands," or "You better be glad I prayed today." I've heard them say, "You gone make me lose my religion!" Such comments reveal what is truly in their heart and subconscious mind. **Nugget:** What's in your subconscious mind, whether good or bad, is what sets the trajectory for your life.

Exercise:

Make a list of all the changes you need to make in your life. For the next 30 days, practice at least one of the new changes you want to make. Please note, to change any old habit or behavior, we must replace it with a new habit. For example, if I want to stop emotionally eating, whenever I want to eat, I must re-program myself to read a book, etc.

_____

_____

_____

_____

_____

_____

_____

_____

_____

_____

_____

Notes...

CHAPTER 6

Silence the Inner Critic

"When there is no enemy within, the enemies outside cannot hurt you."

~ African Proverb

I teach all my clients about the importance of doing "Mindercises", which is the practice of visualization exercises plus affirmations/confessions to see manifestations for permanent positive change. For example, if you want to drop physical weight and develop a new healthier body, you would need to exercise regularly. **Nugget:** Your mind is like a giant muscle. You must commit to re-programming it every day. If you want to drop the mental weight—your old paradigms and negative beliefs, you would also need to do "Mindercises".

I remember when I first started doing my "Mindercises". My old paradigm would try to talk to me. It would say, "You really don't mean what you are saying, and you need to stop lying to yourself." Because I decided to change and was committed, I ignored it and kept on saying the affirmations/confessions. In time, I started believing them, and now they are locked into my subconscious, creating a new healthy mindset. To change permanently and positively, I had to continue my "Mindercises" to develop and walk in my own greatness! I still practice doing them every day.

It has been proven that you feel and act in accordance with what you think or imagine to be true about yourself. Remember, we think, we feel, we act. If you want to change permanently and positively, therefore, you must also do "Mindercises" to re-program how you think and feel about yourself. I say this because that's the only way you will be able to overcome the myriad of voices that will try to prevent you from changing—especially that voice in your head that everyone must confront to move forward and develop the greatness that is within.

Let me explain this a little further. Everyone has an "inner critic," or voice inside their head. Beware because it will often paralyze you from taking any action outside of your comfort zone. This inner critic often makes you feel fearful and unable to move forward.

According to neuroscientists, the desire to develop your greatness and pursue your passion originates in a small area of your brain called the nucleus accumbens. When this part of your brain is activated, the prefrontal cortex part of your brain is triggered, and you instantly start imagining all the possible scenarios that could happen if you were to pursue the desires of your nucleus accumbens, both negative and positive. In other words, your brain was designed by God to prevent and protect you from danger, both emotional and physical. This is also why you are naturally resistant to taking risks.

Unfortunately, this same complex internal system that keeps you from walking in front of a moving car can also prevent you from pursuing/accomplishing your goals. It's designed to help you avoid danger, it tries to prevent you from taking risks, possible embarrassment, and failure. For example, if you decide to start a new business, often the inner critic or voice inside your head will warn you that you might not want to do that because you are not smart enough and will be embarrassed if you fail. Although that voice may be trying to protect you, it can keep you in a state of complacency by telling you that you may not succeed.

When you have an unhealthy mindset—when you are focused primarily on negativity—you program your inner critic to be even far more detrimental. That voice in your head will attack the desires of your heart by attacking you. It will tell you things like you are a loser and start you questioning why you should even bother. If you let it, it will cause you to dwell on your old imperfections and your past, so you will remain stuck, paralyzing you from taking any form of action. In doing so, it robs your self-esteem, leaving you with a bad self-image and a very bad attitude.

You can decide today to stop using your mind as a recorder of your past imperfections and instead start doing your "Mindercises" as a camera lens to see and create your new future. **Nugget:** The best way to predict the future is to create it. Silence that negative inner critic by becoming aware of it and by re-programming an unhealthy mindset with Mindercises about who you are and Whose you are. A healthy mindset refutes and finally silences the inner critic. It will enable you to do as it says in 2 Corinthians 10:5 (NKJV), *"Casting down arguments and every high thing that exalts itself against the knowledge of God, bringing every thought into captivity to the obedience of Christ."*

As it says in this scripture, the way to silence the inner critic is to refute all negative thoughts that are not aligned with who you are and whose you are. Say only what God says about you—not what that negative voice in your head is trying to dictate to keep you stuck.

I remember when I stepped out of my comfort zone and went back to graduate school in my forties. The inner critic in me immediately began telling me that I was too old to go back to college and that maybe I wasn't smart enough to get a master's degree. I silenced that inner critic by doing affirmations that included, *"I can do all things through Christ who strengthens me."* Not only did I earn my graduate degree, but I graduated with a 4.0 GPA.

Once you become aware of the inner critic and learn how to shut it down with the right "Mindercises", you will begin to grow and soar into your destiny while developing in your greatness. I have my "FREE Yourself Confessions & Positive Affirmations" that you can purchase right now at tracyricks.com so that you can begin to move forward and immediately start seeing rapid radical results just like me.

Exercise:

For the next seven days, start paying attention to your inner critic and practice shutting it down. Write down some of your negative self-talk that has been holding you back.

_____

_____

_____

_____

_____

_____

_____

_____

_____

_____

_____

_____

Notes...

CHAPTER 7

Overcome Approval Addiction

"If you live for people's acceptance, you will die from their rejections."

~ LeCrae

I grew up in a family of all girls, nine of us to be exact. You read that right, all females—every single one of us has a different personality—and that makes for a whole lot of different opinions. Perhaps it was because I was number eight in the family and next to the baby that I felt that my older sisters always had the right answers and that I should follow their pattern. I held this belief throughout my high school years until it was time for college.

Most of my sisters graduated from the same historically black college (HBCU). I grew up thinking that I would graduate from high school then automatically follow their path. But when the time came, I knew that I wanted to become a news reporter and was determined to get a degree in broadcast communications. I was disappointed that their university of choice did not offer my major, leaving me without any option but to break from my family's tradition.

I can see now that God used the desire that He had placed in my heart to begin to break me free of my subconscious, self-imposed mindset (paradigm) of thinking that I had to follow their tradition and that I needed my family's approval for anything that I did. But oh, how well I remember hearing jokes about not attending an HBCU. I can now say that I am a very proud alumna of the University of Alabama. Looking back, I know it was a strategic move because it began this very important process in me.

Shifting your old paradigm can require you to be bold and step out of a mold to follow your dreams and visions. Sometimes these "molds" are self-imposed. My family never imposed the path of my older sisters on me. I subconsciously placed *myself* in that container. How? By default—just doing what I saw others around me do—by mostly choosing throughout my childhood just to follow the pattern laid out before me by my older sisters. It wasn't until I made the conscious decision to pursue the dream and vision that I had inside of me that I realized that God's unique plan for my life didn't fit that mold—or anyone else's mold or perceptions of me. Like the Israelites in the Book of Exodus in the Bible, I'd been holding onto a "grasshopper mentality" that would have kept me from entering into what God has for me.

It's a lesson that I've constantly had to re-learn across many areas of my life and over many years. For example, many years ago I decided to go all natural with my hair by letting my relaxer grow out. A lot of people did not agree with my decision, and they were not afraid to voice their opinion about it. I wore braids for a whole year during this journey and because I had the wrong mindset, I was my worst critic. I remember battling with my inner critic that said that my braids made me look "ghetto" (whatever that means) and very unprofessional. I would listen over and over again to a popular song by India Arie, "I Am Not My Hair," almost every day to boost my self-confidence and self-esteem in order to continue my natural hair journey. I can honestly say I am finally free to wear my hair any way I like, without a second thought about what others think or say.

That experience was just part of a process of weaning myself from the need for other people's approval and overcoming my old paradigm with its grasshopper mentality. Seeing this process work in my life caused me to become more aggressive about renewing my mind daily, pursuing my greatness, and getting rid of all those outdated beliefs that were keeping me in bondage. Now, after many years of battling daily with negative thoughts that I just wasn't good enough, pretty enough, or smart enough, I've come to realize that *I am* enough, and I am now walking in my own greatness.

Maybe you're wondering, "What's wrong with wanting to imitate someone else?" That kind of mindset that causes you to want to copy others also may cause you to think small about yourself, which causes you to see yourself small. Seeing yourself as small causes you to dream small—if you even dare to dream at all. You are God's work of art. He created you with the exact nose, facial features, color, and everything else you need to succeed and walk in your own unique greatness! You were made to be unique, and the path that God has for your life is also unique. It's not until you stop trying to look like, act like, talk like, or try to be like someone else—especially others whom we might think highly of, that you will develop your greatness and become your authentic self.

The question you really should be asking yourself is, "Why be a cheap copy of someone else, when you were created to be an amazing original version of your very best self?" In the words of my husband and author, Pastor Rex A. Ricks, Sr., *"There is nothing original about mimicking anyone else... Be yourself!"*

Nugget: May I suggest that instead of trying to mimic or compete with others, learn to embrace your own unique greatness and know that God has enough light for every one of us to shine! I have met so many people in mental bondage and feel pressure to mimic and follow other people's trends. One of the many things I admired about our Former First Lady of the United States, Michelle Obama is she exemplified a self-confident woman who can be used as a reference for others in bondage. The news once reported that she stays away from trends because she likes to do her own thing. As First Lady, she has been praised and admired for "doing her" and having her own style.

I have personally found that when you develop your greatness within and are comfortable in your own skin, you don't feel the need to follow trends. There's nothing wrong with deciding to follow a trend, but you shouldn't be in bondage about having to do things just because someone else is doing it or because you are afraid to step out and be different. Here's a personal example, for years I was in bondage myself believing that I could not wear white after Labor Day. Since shifting my paradigm, I've realized that this is only true for those who believed it to be the truth for them. Now I wear white whenever I like, regardless of whether it's popular with the "trendsetters." My husband is also a great example of someone who is not afraid to "do him", he refuses to follow any type of trend.

Beyond trends, also be careful with social media. So often, many people become dissatisfied with themselves and their present situation after reading about and watching others who appear to "have it all together." A recent study by the Dove Self-Esteem Project (DSEP) revealed that 47% of girls between the ages of eleven and fourteen are suffering from low self-esteem. Low self-esteem is often a result of comparing oneself with others and listening to the negative self-sabotaging thoughts about oneself that come with making such comparisons. Comparing yourself to others either leave you thinking too highly or too lowly of yourself. It can stop you from believing in yourself, making it almost impossible to succeed at anything you attempt.

Is it any wonder that researchers studying the happiness of women in the United States from the 1970s through this present time have found that even though the lives of women have improved drastically, their overall happiness has drastically declined? I discovered that a lot of people, especially women, are not happy with being themselves. This is often due to the pressure of trying to be like and compete with others as a result of entertaining the wrong thoughts and not knowing who you are. When you don't understand that you have greatness within you and you are God's work of art, you will have a hard time being happy with yourself.

I truly believe that developing your greatness and working on becoming your very best self is one of the best gifts that a parent could ever give their child, especially young girls.

"A mother who radiates self-love and self-acceptance actually vaccinates her daughter against low self-esteem."

~ Naomi Wolf

This is another reason why developing your greatness is so important to God—it's not just about you but your generations. Please take a moment now to say this out loud,

"I am predestined to be great, and I never have to imitate or compete with anybody!"

Repeat it over and over. Decide to no longer listen to any self-sabotaging thoughts. The inner critic—that negative, self-condemning voice inside your head—will try to convince you that you're not enough or that you would be enough if only you "looked like" or were "as smart as" someone else that you may admire. Those thoughts are not from God, nor are those thoughts your own. Those thoughts do not serve you well. They are designed to paralyze you, make you doubt yourself, and disregard the greatness that God alone has placed in you for your own benefit and your generations.

In Jeremiah 29:11(NKJV), the Lord assures you that He thinks good thoughts about you and there's no need to seek the approval of others,

"For I know the thoughts that I think toward you, says the Lord, thoughts of peace and not of evil, to give you a future and a hope."

Now, give yourself permission to be unapologetically you and "do you". Take time right now to declare out loud:

"I am fearfully and wonderfully made. I am enough, I am great, and I have everything I need on the inside of me to succeed. I receive God's big plans and purpose for my life."

"Life motivation comes from the deep longings of the heart, and the passion to see them fulfilled urges you onward."

(Proverbs 16:26 TPT)

Exercise:

Write down three unique qualities that you love about yourself and decide to start embracing them.

_____

_____

_____

_____

_____

_____

_____

"I will praise You, for I am fearfully and wonderfully made; Marvelous are Your works, and that my soul knows very well."

(Psalm 139:14 NKJV)

Remind yourself often that in taking the time to change, you are pruning away the habit of being your old self, so you can create a renewed mind to walk in your greatness and start living your very best life.

Notes...

CHAPTER 8

Leave Your Past in the Past

*"The past will continue to be your future if you
drag it along with you."*

~ David Bach

Anna grew up in a family without her dad. After being molested by her mother's boyfriend, she became very promiscuous throughout her teenage years. She had several abortions before the age of 18. During her time in college, Anna met a very nice man. They married and, after several miscarriages, they now have two beautiful children. Anna has a beautiful family and could be happy in her marriage except for one thing: She battles daily with thoughts of her past that keep her from believing she deserves to enjoy life and her new family.

Many people like Anna are allowing their past to keep them from a great future and from enjoying what they do have just because they are unable to forgive themselves and those who hurt them. So the consequences of their misjudgment continue to play out in their lives—far beyond normal recourse. Therefore, they remain a victim.

Just like Anna, you might have made choices that you now regret. Sometimes life throws you a curveball and things happen. Maybe, you didn't see all the ramifications and consequences of your decision before you made it. No one is perfect. In hindsight, you can always see things that you could have done better or maybe done differently. You can't change that, but I have good news, you can decide today that you are going to receive your breakthrough! You don't have to keep punishing yourself or trying to "pay the price." Could all your human effort ever really mend the damage done? No, but guess what? Jesus Christ already took care of it, He took your guilt, shame, and blame.

Did you know that God Himself does not hold your past against you? How can I say that with assurance? Well, the Apostle Paul had a horrible past that included killing Christians. Paul even called himself "the chief among sinners." Yet God still used him in a great way, and he wrote most of the New Testament. King David committed adultery and even had a man killed, but God still called him, "A man after My own heart." Rahab was a harlot, or in today's language she was a prostitute, and God also used her in a mighty way.

If God doesn't hold your past against you, then why should you or anybody else? If God doesn't expect you to be perfect, why should you? Stop allowing things from the past and past mistakes to continue to hold you hostage. Leave your mistakes and heartaches right where they are—in the past. Decide to change what you can change—your future.

Nugget: Your past does not determine your destiny, but your determination to develop your greatness does! No matter what you have done or what might have been done to hurt you, I want to assure you that there is still greatness within you! Even if you have done that one thing that seems unforgivable, your life is still a really big deal to God. You are truly a precious jewel to Him; your life, happiness, and you fulfilling your destiny is a big deal to Him. Your life is a *really* big deal to God.

"I know the plans that I have for you, declares the Lord. They are plans for peace and not disaster, plans to give you a future filled with hope."

(Jeremiah 29:11 GW)

If you're having a hard time embracing your greatness because of mistakes in your past, I can relate. I remember when God began to place a desire on the inside of me to teach people His Word. I began battling with negative thoughts about the things that I'd done in my past and whether I was qualified. I had to convince myself that despite my past, I was good enough with all my flaws that God thought I was to die for, and He would equip me to carry out His purpose for my life.

I remember vividly when I decided to free myself from my past. I began to develop my greatness by re-defining me and finally dealing with my old negative self-image. Almost every day, I would listen to the song, "Imagine Me" by Kirk Franklin, and it helped me change my mindset and shift my paradigm. I would like to share the words of this powerful song with you:

Imagine Me

Loving what I see when the mirror looks at me 'cause I...
I imagine me, in a place of no insecurities
And I'm finally happy 'cause I imagine me
Letting go of all of the ones who hurt me
'Cause they never did deserve me
Can you imagine me?
Saying no to thoughts that try to control me
Remembering all you told me
Lord, can you imagine me?
Over what my mama said
And healed from what my daddy did
And I wanna live and not read that page again

Imagine me, being free, trusting you totally, finally, I can
Imagine me, I admit it was hard to see
You being in love with someone like me
But finally I can Imagine me

Being strong
And not letting people break me down
You won't get that joy this time around
Can you imagine me

In a world (in a world) where nobody has to live afraid?
Because of your love, fear's gone away
Can you imagine me?

Letting go of my past
And glad I have another chance
And my heart will dance
'Cause I don't have to read that page again

Imagine me, being free, trusting you totally, finally I can
Imagine me, I admit it was hard to see
You being in love with someone like me
But finally I can Imagine me

Imagine me, being free, trusting you totally, finally I can
Imagine me, I admit it was hard to see
You being in love with someone like me
But finally I can Imagine me

Gone, gone, it's gone

Every day, we have another opportunity to move forward and make things better. God's mercy is new every morning. Never let anyone tell you that God is holding anything in your past against you. Please don't take that bait. Be assured that He is not mad at you, but madly in love with you! In Isaiah 1:18, the Lord Himself admonishes you to:

"Come now, let's settle this," says the LORD. "Though your sins are like scarlet, I will make them as white as snow. Though they are red like crimson, I will make them as white as wool."

Sometimes people, especially religious people, will try to keep you in bondage about your past. Please hear me clearly, you don't owe anybody an explanation for anything you could have possibly done in your life. Don't let anyone's negative opinion of you become your reality. Just remember what the Bible says—not what others try to say or think about you:

"Therefore, if anyone is in Christ, he is a new creation; old things have passed away; behold, all things have become new."

(2 Corinthians 5:17 NKJV)

I am compelling you to decide to no longer allow your past to define you. **Nugget:** Your past is not you, in fact, God is looking toward you with His loving kindness for He remembers your past mistakes no more:

"For I will be merciful to their unrighteousness, and their sins and their lawless deeds I will remember no more."

(Hebrews 8:12 NKJV)

"He has removed our sins as far from us as the east is from the west."

(Psalm 103:12 NLT)

Anytime someone—especially yourself—tries to condemn you, remind yourself of what God has to say and meditate on His Word:

"Where is another God like you, who pardons the guilt of the remnant, overlooking the sins of his special people? You will not stay angry with your people forever, because you delight in showing unfailing love. Once again you will have compassion on us. You will trample our sins under your feet and throw them into the depths of the ocean!"

(Micah 7:18-19 NLT)

Exercise:

I encourage you to listen to this song and write down anyone or anything from your past that you need to let go and then trash it or burn it, symbolizing your freedom from it. Confess this out loud, "I am now free to believe in me and develop my greatness!"

"Therefore, if anyone is in Christ, he is a new creation; old things have passed away; behold, all things have become new."

(2 Corinthians 5:17 NKJV)

_____

_____

_____

_____

_____

_____

_____

Notes...

CHAPTER 9

Forgive and Heal

"Forgiveness does not change the past, but it does enlarge the future."

~ **Paul Lewis Boese**

W hen you start pursuing your greatness, it may seem difficult to let past hurts caused by others—particularly those you loved or trusted—go. But forgiving is not something you do for those who hurt you, it's something you do for yourself. You may have heard it said that holding on to unforgiveness is like drinking poison but expecting the other person to die. It is so true. Studies have shown that people who forgive are happier and healthier than those who hold resentment. People who forgive tend to have a smaller number of health problems, be less angry, feel less hurt, and are more optimistic. They become more compassionate as well as self-confident.

Forgiving is something you do to free yourself so that you can soar and walk in your greatness.

Nugget: Remember, anything that you are not willing to confront, you are not able to conquer. Despite what they've said, done, or taken from you, you can choose to trust that God has placed everything you need to succeed on the inside of you – regardless of what they have said or done or what you have been through. You owe it to yourself to let that hurt go to move forward and grow.

I knew that I had to be very intentional about walking in forgiveness because I grew up in an environment where people held on to grudges for years—even to the point of not speaking or visiting. I decided when I began to develop my greatness that I would not allow that mentality—often rooted in pride—to keep me from forgiving others. I make daily confessions that I forgive myself and anyone that has ever done me wrong or caused me any harm. I even prayed and sent love out to those same people and declared that I forgave them and all that happened to me until it settled in my heart and became my new reality.

"But I tell you, love your enemies, bless those who curse you, do good to those who hate you, and pray for those who mistreat you and persecute you,"

(Matthew 5:44 WEB)

I had to come to a place of understanding that forgiveness is essential to maintaining healthy relationships. If you choose not to walk in forgiveness, then you will eventually have less meaningful relationships and keep yourself in bondage. At some point or another, every person of significance in your life is going to say or do something that may be hurtful or offensive. Those whom we love have the greatest capacity to hurt us because of the love and openness that we share for and with them—and at times, they are likely to do just that because no one is perfect, not even you and me. Proverbs 27:6 points this out: *"The wounds of a friend are faithful, but the kisses of an enemy are deceitful."*

"Then Peter came to Him and said, "Lord, how often shall my brother sin against me, and I forgive him? Up to seven times?" Jesus said to him, "I do not say to you, up to seven times, but up to seventy times seven."

(Matthew 18:21-22 NKJV)

Having practiced walking in forgiveness for some time now, I can see that too many times, it's not so much hurt but pride that keeps people from forgiving and destroys relationships with loved ones. That's also why it's so very important to pursue the greatness within you and to trust that God has already placed everything you need to succeed on the inside of you despite what other people say or do—even those closest to you who think they know certain things about you and don't have a problem reminding you of them.

In all of this, God has shown me that forgiving yourself is the first step to being able to forgive others. Being unnecessarily hard on yourself and unforgiving creates a mindset and paradigm that eventually causes you to be hard on others and unforgiving of them as well.

Nugget: We cannot give to others what we do not first have ourselves. That's why forgiving yourself is so important to God and to you walking in your greatness.

To help you see the value in forgiving, allow me to clarify that forgiving does not condone the action. I'm not suggesting that what someone else or even yourself did was not wrong and hurtful. Nor am I suggesting that you should continue a relationship with anyone who has caused you harm or that it's okay for you not to change when you may also have been hurtful. Forgiving does not mean forgetting. It is not wise to just blindly disregard what someone is willingly doing that brings harm, leaving you and others susceptible to more pain and heartache. In Matthew 10:16, Jesus Himself admonished His disciples as He sent them out to share the Gospel to,

"Therefore be wise as serpents and harmless as doves."

One awesome thing about forgiveness is that it means that you choose to give up the resentment, revenge, and obsession that comes from what was done and take your power back. Those negative feelings are what contribute to a negative mindset, which is definitely self-destructive and counter-productive to realizing the greatness within you. Forgiveness benefits you and frees you from being a victim to the other person.

Nugget: Forgive so that you can heal! Forgiveness is so important because it focuses your energy on healing, not the hurtful action. It enables you to move from remaining a victim to being victorious in Christ Jesus.

Matthew 6:14-15 admonishes, *"If you forgive those who sin against you, your heavenly Father will forgive you. But if you refuse to forgive others, your Father will not forgive your sins."*

Knowing that you are forgiven brings true lasting freedom and enables you to regain a sense of wholeness and peace. It also turns your attention from the past, enabling you to be present and available to the new opportunities that each day brings. You are now able to fully embrace your greatness with a new attitude.

"Nothing can stop the man with the right mental attitude from achieving his goal; nothing on earth can help the man with the wrong attitude."

~ Thomas Jefferson

I strongly encourage you to begin moving forward today by choosing to forgive yourself and anyone who may have hurt you in the past. Begin to see yourself free from your past. Forgive, let it go, and move forward. Remember, you are re-defining you by forgiving them to "free yourself" so that you can soar and walk in your greatness. **Nugget:** Holding on to unforgiveness, guilt, and condemnation can stop your desired manifestations and keep you in bondage.

Exercise:

List anybody that you need to forgive. Next, take a few minutes and say this out loud: *"I forgive myself and anyone who may have hurt me!"* Last, pray for them and send them love.

_____

_____

_____

_____

_____

_____

_____

_____

_____

_____

_____

_____

_____

Notes...

CHAPTER 10

Connect to the Ultimate Power Source

"I am still far from being what I want to be, but with God's help I shall succeed."

~ **Vincent Van Gogh**

Like most new cars that have GPS that provides direction to your set destination, God has His GPS in you that will lead you to your set destiny in life. You must learn to follow it, even if you do not understand why you should take a certain detour or what appears to be an alternate route. Just learn to trust "His" plan when you cannot trace His hand, knowing that all things are working together for "your" good because your creator is very intentional.

We must stay connected to God as our power source if we plan to continue to follow His GPS for our life. Even a smartphone has maps that will guide you to your set destination. But if that phone is not charged up, it will not work. I have noticed several times throughout a busy day that my phone needs to be recharged. Your life is the same way, you must stay connected and stay charged up to God if you're going to develop your greatness and follow His specific path for your life. Throughout your busy days, you must go back to Him as your power source for clarity and more directions. Everyone has a unique path and God wants to show you the best path for your life. In Psalm 32:8, The LORD says,

"I will guide you along the best pathway for your life. I will advise you and watch over you."

And in Jeremiah 33:3, He tells us:

"Call to me and I will show you great and mighty things you could never figure out on your own."

Here's proof that connecting with God is also very good for our brain. It has been reported that those who connect with God and attend church at least once a month have a 30% to 35% reduced risk of death. Those who attend weekly services are significantly less likely to have a stroke. People who stay connected to God and attend church services frequently are also less likely to smoke, regardless of their denomination. This study followed people for up to 30 years.

Conversely, that same research found that those who randomly attended church services had a higher death rate from digestive, circulatory, and respiratory disorders. Those who felt like they were possessed by demons or experienced spiritual and religious discontent [including feelings that they were being punished by God], had significantly shorter life spans.

This same research determined that fear-based religion is very hazardous to our health. Those focused on fear and guilt—who harbored negative attitudes towards pastors, church members, and especially God—were more inclined to depression and poor health. Those who were angry with God tended to experience more medical issues and generally had very poor recovery rates from hospitalization and from being sick of any form of illness. People who disconnected from God and did not deal with any negative religious issues were especially at risk for bad health and premature death.

What I found most interesting in the results of this study is that people who connect with God and practice daily prayer and meditation for thirty minutes or longer— especially those who have been praying for many years, were shown to have had the greatest benefits in terms of brain functioning and both physical and emotional health.

Apparently, connecting with God through intense prayer and meditation also triggers a very unusual form of neural activity in the brain causing it to ignore negative information sent to it. **Nugget:** During prayer and meditation, you can change and suppress specific negative emotions, while focusing your thoughts in ways that positively influence your mind. Humans are the only creatures on earth that can think themselves into happiness or despair, especially during prayer or meditation.

I encourage you to get connected, stay connected, and let God show you great and mighty things that you could never figure out on your own.

"With God's help we will do mighty things, for He will trample down our foes."

(Psalm 60:12 NLT)

"Those who do wickedly against the covenant he shall corrupt with flattery; but the people who know their God shall be strong, and carry out great exploits"

(Daniel 11:32 NKJV)

Even though I have personally helped many people to discover their life purpose, I've always found that the manufacturer is the "best" source if you want to know the "exact" details about a product. God, our creator, has all the answers we need about our life—and yes, it really is a big deal to Him that you and I develop our greatness within so we can also become our best version of Him!

"For everything, absolutely everything, above and below, visible and invisible, rank after rank after rank of angels—everything got started in Him and finds its purpose in Him."

(Colossians 1:16 MSG)

I can assure you that there is no better counsel outside the counsel of God who created you. I can say that because, after years of being in full-time ministry and being a founding pastor, I became very uncomfortable just watching people who were stuck and unsure about what wasn't working right in their lives. I knew there was more to life than what I was experiencing and seeing in others, but I wasn't even sure what to do to help get results. So I tuned into the GPS that God had placed inside of me and began to seek Him for answers.

While seeking answers, God gave me a desire to become a life coach. I began to follow Valorie Burton and after reading her books, I was led to attend her Coach Training Institute (CTI). It was one of the best decisions I ever made, and was the first step to God bringing me to the point of aggressively shifting my old paradigm for good, facing my fears and becoming more **B.R.A.V.E.**:

- **B-Bold**. Not afraid to stand up and say what needs to be said and do what needs to be done.

- **R-Resilient**. Able to face adversities and bounce back no matter how many times I have setbacks.

- **A-Authentic**. Ready to uncover who I really am by being real and vulnerable with God, myself, and others.

- **V-Virtuous**. Committed to maintaining high morals and standards despite what others may say or think.

- **E-Equipped**. Steadfastly and unapologetically me, living a balanced life, constantly working to become my best self and reach my highest potential, living life on my terms without limits.

Often, we might start off on a particular path, but that doesn't mean that there will not be detours or alternate routes that we need to take along the way to get to our ultimate destination. I started working at a television station immediately after college, even then I knew that particular job was definitely not my final destination. Now, years later, I have transitioned from a pastor to a pastor/life coach, therapist, author and speaker committed to empowering others to also become B.R.A.V.E. In turn, I've been able to help countless people take the journey to realizing their greatness and become the best version of themselves. This is why I can say unequivocally that it is vital that you connect with God – our power source! By staying connected He will also show you His unique blueprint for your life amongst many other great benefits. **Nugget**: The greatness that He has placed on the inside of you is not just for you but will also benefit many others. I have learned that those around us need us to *stay* connected to God to be our unique brand of His given greatness.

Exercise:

Begin to connect with God for at least 15 minutes a day and then begin to write out your vision for your life.

"The Lord confides in those who fear him; He makes His covenant known to them."

(Psalm 25:14 NIV)

Write down what you believe is your God-given purpose.

_____

_____

_____

_____

_____

_____

_____

_____

_____

_____

_____

Notes...

_____

_____

_____

_____

_____

_____

_____

_____

_____

_____

_____

_____

_____

CHAPTER 11

Seek Wise Counsel

"A lot of people have gone further than they thought they could because someone else thought they could."

~ Author Unknown

I want you to know that I believe in you and in your ability to walk in your greatness and live the life you want and deserve. In fact, I'm convinced that living out the greatness that God has placed inside you is *a really big deal* to God! I can say this so definitively because of the transformation that I've made and what I have learned in my own life as well as what I have seen in the lives of others whom God has equipped me to pastor, mentor, and coach.

Take Barbara, for example. She was so full of vision until she married Bob, whom she thought would rescue her from loneliness and debt. But they had four children and Barbara decided to stay at home, creating more debt. Bob remained very active with his hobby of fishing and often spent time with his fraternity brothers. Barbara, on the other hand, felt like it was her responsibility as a mother to stay home and "just be a good wife and mother,"—after all, that's what her mother did and her grandmother before her.

After many years of marriage and raising a family, Barbara began to resent that her husband was enjoying his married life as well as his hobby and friends when she had given up all of her life.

Through counseling, it became clear to Barbara that she can be a good mother and wife and still have hobbies, friends, and even a career. After a short term of coaching and counseling, she's now working her dream job, spending time with her friends, and pursuing her new hobby of painting—while being an awesome mother and an even better wife. As a matter of fact, her relationship with her husband has become much stronger because she is working on "herself" instead of looking to Bob to fulfill the void in her life that she unconsciously created by default. Barbara discovered that she does not have to be a sacrificial lamb for her family. She learned after therapy, it's best if she is not!

I was once like Barbara—unconsciously I put my life and purpose on hold because I wasn't sure how to balance it while being a good wife and mother. I remember feeling like I had been sentenced to motherhood without the possibility of parole, or the option of doing anything else. During that time, we had three small children and two of them were less than two years apart in age. Oh, I can't forget to mention constantly being worried about our newly widowed mother and trying to overcome the unexpected death of our father. I was often frustrated and very irritated. That's also why I was not surprised to learn that it was reported that more men are happier in their marriages than women. I believe it's because a lot of women unconsciously think that they must sacrifice their whole life for their marriage and family, which is untrue. Living the balanced life that you want so that you are happy is key to having a good marriage and creating a great family.

If like Barbara and myself, your old beliefs are no longer serving you—not empowering you to develop your greatness, you must make a choice to replace those beliefs so that you can move forward and start living the life you want. Ask God to bring the right people into your life to help you to do just that. No man is an island to himself. It is very important to have a coach, mentor, pastor—people whom you trust that can help you develop your greatness and fulfill your destiny and purpose in this life.

"Your plans will fall apart right in front of you if you fail to get good advice. But if you first seek out multiple counselors, you'll watch your plans succeed."

(Proverbs 15:22 TPT)

Let me share with you a few key people in my life that God used to help me become the best version of me. My cousin/accountability partner was very instrumental in mentoring me through my transformation to a more balanced living. She would listen, using wisdom to encourage me, and always allowed me to vent. I strongly believe it's very important to have someone you can trust, who will let you "get it out" so that you won't "take it out" on others in your life. Many days, I would share with her my frustrations, concerns, and even my fears of the unknown. She would always let me "get it out" without being judgmental, which is very important. Then she would offer me words of wisdom, that would encourage me to continue to run on and see what the end would be! God would use her, and my breakthrough would come through right on time. She would often say, "Girl, you're going to write a book when you come through this."

My mother-in-love was also a great inspiration while I was transitioning to the life that I wanted. She was—and is—a great example of how a woman of God can support her husband in his ministry while raising 10 children and living a well-balanced life. She, too, would often give me great words of wisdom and encouragement on my journey to developing my greatness.

I truly thank God for all the great women He has placed in my life. I am especially grateful for my mother, who has always been a great example of a strong woman. She is and has always been one of my greatest supporters. She and our father raised nine daughters, sent them all to college, and then went back to school to complete her associate's degree. She has always supported all our dreams and aspirations. Without her support, I would not have become the woman that I am today. And she is the catalyst that inspired me to finish this book.

Also, during my transformation journey, I remember attending a women's conference hosted by Dr. Dee Dee Freeman. I sat in awe as I watched this awesome woman of God in action. I listened to her share how she balanced her fabulous life as a wife and mother while walking out her purpose. I left that conference totally empowered and ready for the changes that I knew that I needed, and that God was encouraging me to make that would push me to develop my greatness and pursue my destiny. Her conference also pushed me to start developing my greatness and pursuing my destiny.

I am so happy that I allowed myself to be mentored/coached and that I have strong, Godly women to support me along my path to developing my greatness. I am now a well-balanced wife, mother, daughter, life coach, therapist, pastor, author, and speaker! I am so very grateful to the great mentors/coaches God placed in my life who have all been good examples that if they did "it," then I can do "it" too. And if "I" can do "it," guess what? So can you. Yes, I also believe in the greatness that God has placed in you too and the importance of you living out your purpose and destiny.

When Seeking A Mentor, Who Do I Choose?

According to the Word of God, a good pastor will equip us spiritually so that we can grow into the things of God. Pastors can equip you to hear from God for yourself and stay connected to Him. But Proverbs 1:5b also says that, *"a man of understanding will attain wise counsel,"*.

"Where there is no counsel, the people fall; But in the multitude of counselors there is safety."

(Proverbs 11:14 NKJV)

A good, anointed coach/mentor can help you with your personal development and also help bring out all the greatness that God has placed inside you. We do this by helping you renew your mind by seeing things differently and help make mid-course corrections so that you can transform and live the life you want. But you must be open to allow your mentor/coach to speak into your life, even if sometimes you might not want to hear it.

"Accepting constructive criticism opens your heart to the path of life, making you right at home among the wise. Refusing constructive criticism shows you have no interest in improving your life, for revelation-insight only comes as you accept correction and the wisdom that it brings."

(Proverbs 15:31-32 TPT)

Please be aware that everybody is not qualified nor authorized to speak into your life. You must also be very careful/prayerful with whom you disclose personal information about yourself and whom you allow to speak into your life. What they say is too important to your overall wellbeing and best interest. So be sure to ask God to lead you to that someone, or lead that someone to you, if you desire a true mentor/coach.

How will you know that you've heard from God regarding the right mentor/coach? There are a few signs that you'll want to see and questions that you'll want to answer about any potential mentor/coach. First, you want to seek out counsel from someone who shares the same values as you: beliefs, ethics, standards—"same spiritual and moral compass." You need to be sure that you can be open, forthright and trust them to provide counsel that aligns with the greatness within you and that agrees with your internal God-given GPS.

Secondly, it's important that this person has proven fruit--evidence of change and greatness in their own life. Can you see in them the very attributes that you are seeking to develop? Have they made the transformation in their life that you are wanting to make? Have they been through similar situations so they can guide you through navigating those uncharted waters in your life?

You also want your mentor/coach to be committed to constantly becoming their own very best self. What are they looking to improve on? You should be able to see this greatness evolving within them. Most importantly—and this is a key indicator—do they have mentors or others to whom they hold themselves accountable?

Of course, the mentor/coach you choose should also be equipped with the tools that you specifically need. Barbara was able to make such fast progress because as her mentor/coach I had her complete a Transactional Analysis that helped Barbara to discover why she believed and thought the way she did. I have found Transactional Analysis to be a very effective tool that many good therapists/coaches use. Similarly, I have developed a course, the exact system I used for my transformation, for permanent positive change, that I walk through with all my clients. You need to ask how a good mentor/coach will work with you to develop the greatness within you, what measurements do they have in place to track your growth?

Your mentor/coach must have the ability to be frank and honest with you in giving you feedback and guidance. Are they able to offer you constructive advice? Notice that I said, "constructive advice." As already discussed, what we don't need is criticism. You want someone who will tell you the truth in a way that you can receive it—especially when you may not necessarily want to hear it. If they make you feel less about yourself, they are not the mentor/coach for you. If they cannot help you face your fears, they are not the mentor/coach for you.

Most importantly, before making your decision, ask yourself, "Does this person inspire me? Do they see and believe in the greatness within me?" **Nugget:** You want a coach/mentor whom you can safely trust, meaning they have both the ability and the intent to have your best interests at heart. It's not enough for someone to want to be able to help you. They also must be equipped to see and help you develop your specific greatness. That's the difference between your friends and a mentor/coach—the right mentor/coach.

I've seen the negative impact that well-meaning friends and family—even so-called mentors and coaches—

can adversely have. Let me tell you about Natalie, a 35-year-old CEO of a thriving company. To many people, Natalie has "it" all together. She's at the top of her career game. But Natalie doesn't have a social life because of the long days she spends working. She thought she would be married at this point in her life and is starting to resent having given up her social life and desires to have a family for what "appears" to be a fabulous career. She often dreams about starting her own business as an interior decorator, which is what she wanted to do but her dad told her many times during her high school years that she needed a secure career that provides a great income. Her father "coached" and advised her to choose what was safe but has proven to be very unfulfilling. She is limiting her greatness, feeling stuck, and very unhappy.

I have met numerous people who are very similar to Natalie. They are reluctant to step out on their instincts and the desires within them—their greatness within—because of what loved ones, friends, guidance counselors, and even well-meaning pastors have said. Pray and ask God for His guidance concerning who you need to choose. Also, commit to first allow your pastor to become your spiritual parent/guidance. Next, be prayerful and let God help you choose the best mentor/coach to guide you on your unique path to your unique purpose awaiting you.

"For the wisdom of the wise will keep life on the right track..."
(Proverbs 14:8a TPT)

Exercise:

Write down at least three people you would like to have as a mentor or coach in your life and set a date to connect with them. (Even if only through videos or social media.)

_____

_____

_____

_____

_____

Pray and ask God for His guidance concerning who you need to choose. Also, commit to allowing your pastor to become your spiritual parent/guidance.

Notes...

CHAPTER 12

Stay Ready to Pursue and Possess

"There is a difference between wishing for and being ready to receive it."

~ **Napoleon Hill**

Have you heard of the 90/10 rule of planning? It says that the first 10% of the time that you spend planning and organizing work before you begin saves you as much as 90% of the time necessary to get the whole job done.

For every great plan and purpose in your life, there are seasons of preparation. I now know that I am called to empower people all over the world to live their best lives and become the best version of themselves. But there were times when my first responsibility was to develop my relationship with my husband, my children, and most of all my relationship with myself. I know you are probably thinking, didn't she say that you don't have to be a sacrificial lamb for your family? Yes, you are right, but I also knew the importance of maintaining order and balance to see good, Godly results while developing my greatness.

There was a season in my life when God placed a desire in my heart to stay home and home-school our kids. This was also a time of developing me as a helpmeet to my husband and a better mother to our children. It was during that time of preparation that my greatness was *really* starting to develop. Oh boy, was there a lot of pruning and shaking going on in my life. It was the best of times, but it often seemed more like the worst of times. I had to learn, having a total paradigm shift, that it was no longer about just me and my wants, needs, and desires.

Even though I knew my husband loved me and my family loved me too, only God could give me the specific answers I needed for my personal and spiritual growth during those times. I would frequently battle with negative thoughts about not being good enough, crying out to God, while also seeking encouragement from my mentors, and spending much time alone in prayer. Today I am a stronger and better mother, wife, pastor, coach, and friend because I didn't let it break me. I allowed that "fire" to make me a better person as I learned how to develop my greatness. In the words of Whitney Houston, "I didn't know my own strength." This strength, of course, was rooted in God.

Notice that I used the word "fire," in reference to my seasons of preparation? Diamonds are refined through the pressure of the fire. If you're going through some fire right now, keep on growing through it and let it redefine you. If you do, your fire can shape and develop you into the greatest person that you are called to be.

"In the same way that gold and silver are refined by fire, the Lord purifies your heart by the tests and trials of life."

(Proverbs 17:3 TPT)

Maybe in this season you are single and desiring to be married. Learn to be happy with yourself, learn to enjoy being by yourself. Marriage was never meant to be a cure for loneliness—just ask some of your married friends. Nor was marriage meant to rescue you from debt. The only person who can truly rescue us already did that on the cross and His name is Jesus!

During your single years, maybe prepare yourself for marriage by clearing any old debts and avoiding unnecessary new ones. Take advantage of this time to become whole by spending countless hours working on you and spending time with your Creator. God is all about you being prepared to walk in your destiny and purpose without delay. Developing your greatness and becoming the best version of you during this season is essential for having a successful marriage.

"Know the importance of the season you're in and a wise son you will be..."

(Proverbs 10:5 TPT)

Beyond my relationships with my husband, children, and myself, I also had a season of preparation specific to my calling to empower others. I knew that before I could empower anybody else, I had to learn how to empower myself. I found out that anyone can give advice, but it takes a strong, mature person to use it on themselves first. Please note that preparation involves enduring, learning, and applying principles/the Word of God during the good, bad, and even the ugly events in our life. It can be painful at times, requires lots of work, dedication, and education.

Just think about it: Would you want a doctor who has never been to medical school to operate on you? Would you hire a lawyer who never went to law school? It's during the many years of learning that doctors and lawyers are prepared to be effective in their profession. Jesus Christ Himself prepared for years to fulfill His purpose.

You, too, cannot expect to do great things if you fail to prepare during the seasons when maybe no one knows your name and you don't have a great following. I often see people who want to rush to do the next "big thing," when they do not have the character to keep them while doing even the "little thing." The Word of God teaches us that if we are faithful over few things, then He will make us rulers over many. Don't allow yourself during this time of preparation to feel insignificant.

"Until you are ready to look foolish, you'll never have the possibility of being great."
~ Cher

Decide to remain committed without allowing yourself to grow weary while doing good. Get ready and stay ready because your due season is coming, and you want to be ready and well prepared!

"Go to the ant, you sluggard! Consider her ways and be wise, which, having no captain, overseer or ruler, provides her supplies in the summer, and gathers her food in the harvest."

(Proverbs 6:6-8 NKJV)

As Benjamin Franklin has been quoted as saying, "If we fail to prepare, we prepare to fail." Just imagine the success you will see in your life once you start applying this 90/10 rule!

Once you are prepared, there will come the time to pursue and possess all the great things that God has for you and start walking in your greatness. You will know it's time because you no longer need anyone to validate you. You no longer need the approval of others. You will see the obstacles in your life as the steppingstones to your success that they truly are. You can no longer be denied or deterred. Why? Because you decided to redefine you and start walking in your new freedom!

"So if the Son makes you free, then you are unquestionably free."

(John 8:36 AMP)

The verse above is one of my favorite Scriptures because it helped liberate me and pushed me into my purpose. I am now free to be uniquely me and walking in my greatness.

Be aware that you will also likely experience fear, which is caused by the terror barrier. I know because as I stepped out into pursuing my purpose and began writing this book, I heard loud and clear, "Brave women do it afraid." In other words, despite those feelings of fear of the unknown, go ahead, step out in faith, and just do it. I had no idea what it would take to write, publish, or distribute a book. All I knew was that I must write this book for people like you to learn that you have greatness already in you and that your life really does matter to God.

Often times you and I just need a little extra knowledge and coaching to be empowered to pursue that greatness. And sometimes you just have to take that leap and push yourself out of your comfortable nest. Just know that once you decide to step out and pursue your greatness, there will be the terror barrier – designed to stop you from continuing your journey by causing you to feel afraid. But please go ahead and do it afraid, choosing to keep moving forward.

What is it that you love to do? What's holding you back from walking in it and living out your dreams and vision? Keep your eye on that prize and seek the wise counsel that you may need to support yourself. You can do it! I know that you can. That's why I've written this book— to let you know that you are predestined for greatness! I'm a living witness that you were created on purpose, for a specific purpose.

Many of us have decided to step out and do it afraid. Now it's your time! Step out of the boat, jump out of the box, and blow it up! It's normal and okay to be shaky and nervous and feel inadequate. Just know that you got this, and God got you! Your Creator loves you so much, and He will never leave you nor forsake you. You are not alone or outnumbered. You plus God are the majority!

Your wait is now over. Decide that today is the day for your breakthrough! Walking in your destiny and developing your greatness is assured because your Creator is on your side and developing the greatness that He has placed uniquely within you is a very big deal to Him. So take a few minutes right now to rejoice and celebrate your greatness because you have the victory. The verdict is in and you win! **Nugget:** Winning is a part of your spiritual DNA—it goes with what God has already placed in you.

I encourage you to be like Carla, who knew as a child that she loved to work with numbers. Throughout school, she loved math. When she went to college, she earned a degree in accounting. She worked for an accounting firm for many years until she started desiring to own her own firm. What did Carla do? She went back to school to take more courses focused on running a business. After a few additional years of preparation, she knew it was time to step out on her vision. She faced her fears and opened her own firm. Carla was determined and therefore could not be denied, despite the challenges that came with opening her own business. She is now very successful and more fulfilled. All because she decided to go past the terror barrier by facing her fears and embracing her greatness.

Trust me, I am a witness, there is no greater joy than developing your greatness, becoming the best version of you and walking in your God-given purpose and destiny.

Exercise:

List some areas where you feel like you are being prepared right now.

_____

_____

_____

_____

_____

_____

_____

_____

_____

_____

_____

_____

Notes...

CHAPTER 13

Never Give Up!

"Our greatest weakness lies in giving up. The most certain way to succeed is to always try just one more time"

~ Thomas Edison

It's never too late to be great. Today, I want you to begin embracing the new redefined you with a new mindset that says, "I am great, and I can achieve anything I want no matter what it takes or how hard it may appear." Obstacles are going to come but refuse to give up, no matter what. Decide to shift your paradigm and never look back.

Many of the world's greatest success stories took overcoming the many obstacles along the way. Albert Einstein did not speak until he was four years old and could not read until he was seven; his parents and teachers thought he was mentally handicapped. He also failed his college entrance exam. Abraham Lincoln lost 26 political campaigns before winning public office. Author, J. K. Rowling went from welfare to becoming one of the richest women in the world after five years of hard work and determination. Walt Disney was fired for "lacking imagination" and having no good ideas. Colonel Sanders of Kentucky Fried Chicken was rejected by more than a thousand restaurants and his recipe for fried chicken is now famous. Thomas Edison was told that he was "too stupid to learn anything." It took him more than a thousand attempts at inventing the light bulb, yet he persevered. He didn't let what others said about him or even what could be perceived as a failure to stop him. When asked why he didn't give up, Edison said that he did not fail once but discovered over a thousand things that did not work. Michael Jordan was cut from his high school basketball team. Countless people remained consistent and persistent despite the many adversities. If we plan to succeed, we too must develop the strength of character that's committed and refuse to give up, no matter what, because our life success and walking in our greatness matters—it's a really big deal to God and should be a big deal to you and me too.

If you knew that you had a guarantee that whatever you pursued concerning your destiny would succeed, what would you begin to do? **Last Nugget:** God has given you a guarantee that everything you set your hands to do will prosper.

"Turn to the LORD for help in everything you do,
and you will be successful."
(Proverbs 16:3 ERV)

So go for it and know that you are not alone. As President Franklin Delano Roosevelt infamously said, "The only thing we have to fear, is fear itself." It's your time to shine and start living your very best life—the life that you want and deserve! Begin to rise to your highest potential and run into your destiny with confidence, knowing that your life and walking in your greatness is truly a really big deal to God and ME!

I have one last closing remark as our time together is coming to an end. Once upon a time I did not know that I was born with greatness already inside of me. After learning whose I am, I decided to develop my greatness by daily empowering myself to shift my paradigm—and that's when I began to redefine me and started living my very best life. My prayer is that you also will decide to commit to a total paradigm shift while also developing your greatness, realizing that there are no limits in God.

Thank you for allowing me to share my transformation journey with you and this book was written to help develop your greatness and take every area of your life to the next level, even faster than you may have ever thought possible. And if you are really ready to take your life to a whole new level, I would love to coach you in my life-changing online course, "I'm Ready Now!!!" Level 1, Level 2, or Level 3. Visit tracyricks.com for more information and to check for openings.

Now that you have labored to develop your greatness by transforming and putting your mind in a healthy place, my prayer is that you enter into God's rest in the finished work of Jesus Christ! Always remember, while He was hanging on the cross, Jesus said, "it is finished", so now you can have a fresh start in life. Selah

~Your TheraCoach, Tracy Ricks

"There remaineth therefore a rest to the people of God. For he that is entered into his rest, he also hath ceased from his own works, as God did from his. Let us labour therefore to enter into that rest, lest any man fall after the same example of unbelief."

(Hebrews 4:9-11 KJV)

Prayer of Salvation to Receive Jesus: (say this out loud)

Jesus, I receive You as my personal Lord and Savior. I thank You for a fresh new start in life. I repent of my sins and now give my life to You. Today, I choose to walk in my greatness and embrace the new life You obtained for me.

"that if you confess with your mouth the Lord Jesus and believe in your heart that God has raised Him from the dead, you will be saved. For with the heart one believes unto righteousness, and with the mouth confession is made unto salvation."

(Romans 10:9-10 NKJV)

Say this prayer out loud:

Now Father, I take authority over every spirit that's not of you, that have held me back in my past and stopped me from walking in my greatness. Today, I receive my newness of life provided by the finished works of Jesus Christ. I have taken off my old man and put on my new man who has been totally renewed in Your image. I am now free and walking in my FULL deliverance! **I will never be the same in Jesus Name, Amen.**

Exercise:

Decide to now maintain the great new life Jesus obtained just for you. Write out in detail the new redefined you and the new beginning for your new, great, balanced life.

_____

_____

_____

"My old identity has been co-crucified with Messiah and no longer lives; for the nails of his cross crucified me with him. And now the essence of this new life is no longer mine, for the Anointed One lives his life through me—we live in union as one! My new life is empowered by the faith of the Son of God who loves me so much that he gave himself for me, and dispenses his life into mine!"

(Galatians 2:20 TPT)

Notes...